Malcolm Garrett is a retired English and History teacher who spent the last twenty-nine years of his career as Head of English at Brisbane State High School. In that role, he keenly promoted Australian literature—especially Australian poetry.

Malcolm has written a number of English textbooks, the most recent, *English Toolkit Ed 2: The Nuts and Bolts of English Grammar*, being a section winner in the 2016 Australian Educational Publishing Awards. During the height of the COVID-19 pandemic, he worked with his daughter to program an interactive version of that grammar text, which can be found at https://englishtoolkit.xyz/.

The downing of MH17 on 17 July 2014 was a life-changing event for Malcolm and Liz, with the loss of Liz's sister Jill and brother-in-law Roger. The two couples had just finished a river cruise from Budapest to Amsterdam followed by two delightful days in Bruges, when they went separate ways— Malcolm and Liz to Paris and Jill and Roger to board the ill-fated flight home from Amsterdam. In wrestling with their loss, Malcolm found solace in writing poetry. In the years that followed, he also turned to poetry to express his joy at being a grandfather and to reflect on current issues.

Malcolm and Liz now live on the Sunshine Coast, near their son and his family.

In loving memory of Jill and Roger Guard.

Malaysian Airlines Flight MH17 was shot down over Ukraine on 17 July 2014—a casualty of the civil war going on there. Among the victims were my wife's sister Jill and brother-in-law, Roger. The flight had left Schiphol Airport in Amsterdam and a large number of the passengers were Dutch. The poem that gives its title to this anthology was written on the occasion of the opening of the National Monument to the victims, which monument is situated in Park Vijfhuizen near Schiphol Airport and was opened on 17 July 2017, the third anniversary of the tragedy. The photo below was taken on that day.

Malcolm Garrett

ANTHOLOGY: A WOW OF SUNFLOWERS

Moving on After MH17

AUSTIN MACAULEY PUBLISHERS™

LONDON * CAMBRIDGE * NEW YORK * SHARJAH

A CIP catalogue record for this title is available from the British Library.

ISBN 9781035832675 (Paperback)
ISBN 9781035832682 (ePub e-book)

www.austinmacauley.co.uk

First Published 2024
Austin Macauley Publishers Ltd®
1 Canada Square
Canary Wharf
London
E14 5AA

I would like to thank my immediate and extended family for allowing me to share our story in this public space.

Table of Contents

About This Anthology

I have always been enchanted by the power of words to encapsulate human experience, which no doubt explains why I became an English teacher. However, during a busy life as head of an English department in a large secondary school, most of my poetry had either been to model poetic genres for students or to celebrate a family birthday or a colleague's retirement—occasional poetry in its strictest sense. All that changed on 17 July 2014 with the downing of flight MH17.

My wife Liz and I had just completed a wonderful cruise from Budapest to Amsterdam with my wife's sister Jill and her husband Roger—one of the happiest times of our life. The four of us had added on a couple of days in the delightful canal city of Bruges before Liz and I farewelled Jill and Roger on Ghent railway station. Liz and I were extending our holiday by going on to Paris and the Somme, to visit a family war grave. Jill and Roger returned to Amsterdam to board the ill-fated flight MH17.

Both the love of family and the loss of loved ones are poignant sharpeners of a poet's pen. Particularly since that event have I turned to poetry both to wrestle with loss and to celebrate joy. A particular joy has been the joy that grandchildren bring.

I hope that this anthology will help you deal with loss, celebrate joy and reflect on issues in the way that writing the poems has helped me.

Malcolm Garrett, 2023

A Wow of Sunflowers

There are different kinds of 'wow'.
There is the simple admiration of
"Wow! What a backhand!"
or "Wow, what a big steak!"
or "Wow, what a beautiful woman!"
There is the gleeful wow of
having a seat allocation
in the emergency exit row
with room to uncoil long legs!
Ah! Wow!
Then, of course, there is awe at
300 tonnes of aeroplane
effortlessly rising into the sky:
pure physics in action.
Awesome! Wow!
…but then there is something beyond wow:
there is the audible gasp of the choir as our bus
rounded a corner in Kyoto in the middle of a rainy night,
rain scudding across the face of a spot-lit pagoda!
Oh wow!
or the jaw-dropping sight of Iguassu Falls
or Victoria Falls

or Iceland's Skógafoss:
power and beauty intertwined!
Wow! Wow!
Or my heart stopping the first time I heard Allegri's
Miserere
with a boy soprano rising from middle C to top C,
effortlessly, time and again.
Wow upon wow!
And beyond wow was the wow of
being embraced by a wow of sunflowers
on entering the MH17 memorial at Vijfhuizen Park;
and a new-born baby defying the
depths of despair in the profound silence
of a sombre roll-call of two-hundred and ninety-eight names
with her beautiful, insistent life-affirming cry!

17 July 2017

Wrestling with Loss

Sunflowers in Ukraine

In sunflower fields their bodies lie;
No doubt a pretty place to die
Assuming nature lovers must
Like everybody come to dust.

Her hug is warm upon my breast,
His vital palm upon my palm.
How could unfeeling fate conspire
To bring them to such senseless harm?

No cause can justify such pain!
No righteous stance, no grander plan
Absolves the crimes of callous men:
Man's inhumanity to man.

Oh may the sunflowers in Ukraine
Turn callous hearts so they can see
That love alone has moral force
And live in peace and harmony.

But as for us who mourn them now
If we see yellow sunflowers grow

Our hearts will miss a beat and say
It's time for us to let them go;
Though every fibre of our souls
Will wish and wish it were not so.

July 2014

Sunflowers from Ukraine

In sunflower fields their bodies lay
Already starting to decay
Till loving hearts arrived for them
To take them back to Eindhoven.

One journalist was there and knew—
And this was his epiphany—
That suffering and grief and loss
Are deeper than a front-page story.

What could he do? The dead were dead!
To act, to change—beyond his powers.
Nigh on three hundred bodies strewn;
The only life was in the flowers.

He could do nothing for the dead
Except report their tragic fate.
All that was living were the flowers;
Could these salve hearts fair fit to break?

He gleaned some seeds and brought them back
And even though our hearts will know

Loved ones are gone alack! alack!
We'll plant those seeds and watch them grow
And doing so perhaps acquire the knack
To hold them close but also let them go.

*with sincere thanks to journalist Paul McGeough and
photographer Kate Geraght*

17 July 2015

Five Years On

What is a number but one more
Than whatever number comes before;
And so with time the years condense
And in a very real sense
If we count backwards minus one
And minus one and minus one,
We very soon are back to where
You and I were such a lucky pair!

So numbers lose significance:
Just as we feel His immanence
Whatever point we're at in time!
So I am yours and you are mine
You loved me deeply that I know
And still I bask in that love's glow
For though your body is no longer here,
Our souls will ever be entwined, my dear.

Written for cousin Dot on the fifth anniversary
of the loss of her beloved husband Ken

The Second Cat

Only cat lovers will really understand what I mean
when I say: *She is a cat lover!*
Silently, tales aloft, cats enter a room
imperiously commanding attention;
and cat lovers' hearts jump to attention.
Come my way, kitty.
Let me pay homage!
Let me be the one to stroke you
from head to tip of that imperious tail
In hope of evoking your beatific feline largesse:
The inner rumbling of 'an enclosed and private sound'
stilling my heart
in serene peace.
OM!

She is a cat lover.
In her room in the nursing home
feline artefacts, gifts from the family,
for years have elevated her spirits.
On the shelf under the TV, directly in front of her recliner,
four ceramic cats, four different colours,

tails proudly aloft, parade across a shelf
constant iconic reminders of four beloved daughters
equally proud, equally adored.
OM!

She is a cat lover;
but this morning something is wrong:
the second cat is lying on its side,
no tail in the air, no walking tall and proud.
Why isn't it standing? she wonders. Panic sets in,
an intense feeling that something bad has happened:
something bad has happened to daughter number two!
On the TV, the focus is on the search for missing bodies
in a field of sunflowers in Ukraine.
Her body shudders; memories rise to the surface
through the treacle of her dementia until
on this morning, as on so many previous mornings
she deals afresh with the tragic news
that daughter number two was on
MH17!

A carer arrives, suggests a change of channel,
Busies herself tidying the room…but she knows,
as she does every other morning,
that the second cat has a sad, daily job to do
and must remain lying on its side!

Splinters

An open fireplace gets little use
in Queensland, where, the slogan says,
it's beautiful one day; perfect the next—
except today; oh what a dismal day:
a day to split some timber
and light a fire for a cat to stretch in front of;
a fire to warm a fraught heart,
while Allegri's ethereal *Miserere Deus*[*]
hovers at divine heights above the crackling flames:
Have mercy on me, O God—
and on all humanity.

From the wood pile, I select the best of firewood
1940s vintage logs from house stumps
salvaged from restumping Nick's house.
No smoke from these dried-out stumps;
just golden embers…
for today I seek purity:

---

[*] Psalm 51

Make me a clean heart, O God,
and renew a right spirit within me.
Ouch! A splinter!

I should wear gloves, I know,
but there is something about handling the timber
before it is sacrificed in the flames…

Ah! splinters in my hand give little pain
compared to piercing splinters in my heart and brain;
for splintered too was MH17 two years ago:
man's inhumanity to man has laid me low.

Purge me with hyssop and I shall be clean…!
Then shall I teach Thy ways unto the wicked:
and sinners shall be converted unto Thee.

17 July 2016

Empty Rooms
on Settlement Day

Well, settlement is only hours away;
The house will not be ours by end of day.
So here we are for one quick final check
That every room's been left both span and spick.

How strange it is to walk each empty room
Nothing remains but four bare walls—a tomb;
Yet if we stand and listen, we can hear
A symphony of memories loud and clear.

Here a little girl would twirl and prance
Delighting in the rhythm of the dance;
And here a little boy would don team colours
'Cos his team mattered more than all the others.

And here a little girl drew curtains back
So she could thrill to each loud thunder crack;
And here a little boy slept with his boots on
So he'd be ready for his soccer game next morning!

And bath time was a time of special joy
With Daddy home from work at end of day;
And he would supervise the children's bath
While everyone would splash and play and laugh.

But bedtime stories were the very best
We'd cuddle close, a bedtime story nest;
And teddy had to be there to hear too
Of Piglet, Eeyore, Tigger and of Pooh.

It's time to go, there's no more time to linger
Although our hearts yearn to remain much longer.
Your day of settlement has come and you depart
How empty yet how full—your room within my heart!

Written after the death of my brother, John

Lilac Days

The breeder told us take a seat
And watch the Burmese kittens play
Something I could have done all day
But we had a mission to complete.

Which of the kittens would we choose?
But that, she said, was not the way;
The cats, it seemed, must have a say!
Well…if one chose me, I'd not refuse!

And sure enough a lilac kitty
Jumped on my lap as if to say
Get used to it; I'm here to stay
And groomed herself quite happily.

For fourteen years to my delight,
She kept me company by day
(Except when she went out to play)
And curled up on my legs at night;

Or maybe burrowed down the bed
On winter nights when it was cold
(Warming my feet—how could I scold?)
Her happy purr infused my head.

But now, oh my, oh me, oh meow
No more, no more will she resound
With her enclosed and private sound,
Oh me, oh my, oh me, oh meow.

Written after the death of
my beautiful lilac Burmese cat, Lucinda

Three Score Years and Ten

It was always going to be too short, the time we had together;
Would it have been enough for us if it had been for ever?
But that is not the hand we're dealt, though this I know is true:
Whatever moments I have had, I'm glad they were with you!

Oh no, I will not kid you; I'll be honest with myself!
I'd really hoped there would be time for one more round of golf,
To hear the crisp connection of the golf ball and the club
And see it land upon the green; but sadly here's the rub:

I've had my threescore years 'n ten—perhaps I can't complain!
I've watched my children growing up and shared their joys
      and pain
And blessed is the man, it's said, who sees his children's
      children;
But think of all the 'might've beens' lymphoma has now stolen!

Well, I'm not deeply religious; it has never been my way.
I have no special wisdom here, but one thing I can say:
This is the hand that I've been dealt, and this I know is true:
Whatever moments I have had, I'm glad they were with you!

33

Our Enigmatic Steve

I've tried to write a poem but the words struggle to come;
You threw your precious life away and that has left us numb.
It must have taken courage or was it pure despair
'Cos we're living in a universe that doesn't seem to care?

Or was it simply chemistry, a mental illness glitch,
A fate destined within the genes, which really is a bitch!
Do we control our choices or is free will just a con?
Well, maybe now you know at last; you've crossed the
      Rubicon!

You tried to make some sense of it, what life is all about,
Though philosophers before us have all failed to work it out!
You didn't find the answers in a temple, mosque or church;
If God exists, it seems quite clear he left *you* in the lurch.

You would have saved the rainforests, wiped tears from every
      eye;
You would have saved the children like the catcher in the rye.
Yet for some obscure reason you thought you bore the mark
      of Cain:
A burden of distorted guilt the centre of your pain.

Oh, Steve, you came quite close to solving life's enigma—
If only you had not attached to passion some dark stigma!
The only thing that matters to make sense of life's brief span
Is to *love* another person and to *be loved* in return.

And so farewell, our gentle Steve, you enigmatic soul;
We'll not forget your gentle laugh, your enigmatic smile.
Now at last your tortured heart can find a tranquil peace;
The constant turmoil in your brain can now for ever cease.

Written after the suicide of a gentle but tormented nephew
who had been suffering from schizophrenia

A Ray of Jamaican Sunshine

A Ray of Jamaican sunshine was my neighbour Mamma Merle:
She warmed all those around her; even halfway across the world
My cousin in Australia felt something of her power
Through a photo of her standing in her garden near a flower.

It was the biggest sunflower that you will ever see;
And sunflowers are a symbol for a shattered family
Still reeling from the sudden loss of loved ones in Ukraine
Where a field of sunflowers was the scene of the downing of
      a plane.

And that was Mumma Merle, you see; she spread her love
      around:
She stood with us and gave her strength through gestures
      quite profound.
She stood beside me through my grief at losing husband Ken
And I had cause to bless her for her strength time and again.

In Africa are little girls dressed in cute frocks she made
Just one example how she sought to give the needy aid.
She was a ray of sunshine and although she's passed away
The sunshine of her memory will help to light my way.

37

Little Legs

Celebrating
Grand Children

The Gift of Language

In the beginning, there are no words,
just an amorphous collection of gurgles—
and cries, of course;
happiness and distress
wrapped in a confused burbling pudding.

Slowly, gradually, focus begins:
First there is the naming!
Did he say, "Da Da"?
I'm sure he said, "Mumma"!
'Nan Nan' comes early for milk is life's staple;
And who doesn't like 'cado'!
"Muh pease!"—nothing wrong with his manners!

And nothing wrong with his sight or hearing!
"Buh" draws our attention to birds.
"Copter" he says, pointing to a distant speck in the sky
…and ambulances are fun: "Nee Nah Nee Nah".

Neither is he colour blind,
for 'lellow' can be differentiated from 'porple'
green traffic lights from red
with orange lights winking in between.

Suddenly, epiphany: words can be combined!
lellow digger
tip-up truck
big one

Adjectives and nouns combined—
Oh, it is easy to see where
a young man's interests lie!

Suddenly, epiphany: words can be pre-positioned!
IN here, he says as he fills the ark with animals
OVER legs, he says as he scrambles over Grandad's legs
UP high, he says as Daddy lifts him high in the air
UNDER table, he says as he crawls into his cubby
OUT door, he says as he pleads to go outside

…and post-positioned:
Standing UP, he says as he balances his toy figures
Lid ON, he says as he puts the lid on the little teapot

And in a grammatical flourish, the verbs appear
and sentences emerge:
Dan Dan zip, he says as he struggles to unzip the laptop case
Dan lid on, he says as he puts the lid on the Thermomix
Daddy sit here, he says, as he pats the lounge beside him.

Thus begin all poets.
Soon, soon, with a flourish of verbal legerdemain,
he will be telling
of his spring-walks-in-the-Black-Forest lightness of heart;
of a beauty so rare it is wont to launch a thousand ships;
and of a love so deep he will reach out
and lay his quivering heart in his lover's trembling hand!

First Steps

Young Daniel is walking; he can take a few steps.
He waddles along with hands fully outstretched.
He's clearly delighted; he has a big grin.
He can tell from our clapping we are happy with him!

So he claps himself too, which can bring him undone
And he ends up *post haste* plopping down on his bum.
But that doesn't faze him; he straightaway stands
This time with a big rubber ball in his hands.

But now and again he reverts to the floor
Walking like a koala, raised up on all four
Of his strong little limbs; it's a quick way to go
And he squeals as he races Big Sis to and fro.

Oh, millions of babies have done this before
But our gaze is on *this* one; he's ours to adore.
One wonders to whither these first steps will lead;
The journey's begun and we wish him God speed!

Chefs Cordon Bleu

Grandma is cooking and Amber is helping
Up on the benchtop, her little legs dangling
They read from a recipe what to put in
And gather ingredients before they begin.

Add two cups of this and a spoonful of that
And of course all the while there's a lot of chit chat
And a lot of taste testing appears to ensue:
An absolute must for young chefs cordon bleu!

It could be a pizza—avocado, cucumber—
A special design of chef cordon bleu Amber
Or maybe choc spiders since it's Halloween
Or the fanciest cupcakes that you've ever seen.

Grandma is cooking and Amber is helping:
She is turning the dial and adjusting the setting.
All is ready to go, so she puts on the lid
'Cos Amber's a four-year-old Thermomix kid!

Uh-Oh!

Humpty Dumpty sat on a wall
But Humpty Dumpty had a great fall:
Uh-oh!
The little man's reading a book he has found
And points and exclaims at smashed egg on the ground:
Uh-oh!

Little man's reading a book in the car;
It slips from his knees and falls onto the floor:
Uh-oh!
And if he is eating a treat or a snack
Somehow all the bikkies end up in his lap!
Uh-oh!

Little man hums with his red spinning top
'Til churlish inertia brings top to a stop!
Uh-oh!
It wobbles and wobbles and wobbles some more
And then it flops onto its side on the floor:
Uh-oh!

Little man likes to slip down a long slide
But doesn't like sand at the end of the ride:
Uh-oh!
He rubs hands together to brush off sticky sand;
It really is more than a poor boy can stand!
Uh-oh!

Little man grins while Grandad and Grandma
Make a big domino snake on the floor:
Uh-oh!
When they are ready, he gives one a push:
All of the dominoes fall with a crash!
Uh-oh!

Little man presses the tv remote
With little idea what the buttons denote:
Uh-oh!
And then when he finds that the picture has gone,
He looks up at Grandad; they say with a grin:
Uh-oh!

Cupcake

On Grandfather's lap, a one-year-old boy
Is eating a cupcake with obvious joy.
A wide chocolate border encircles his mouth
And crumbs are strewn everywhere over the couch!

His eyes are attentive because on the top
Are little white pieces; sweet marsh mellow drops
And Grandad makes sure that with each piece he breaks
A marshmallow droplet is part of that flake!

Now Grandad is patient and waits till he's sure
That each mouthful's finished so he'll hear the word 'Muh!'
With an upturned inflection; the one-year-old knows
With absolute certainty which way the wind blows!

At the end of the treat, Grandad tells him, "All gone"
And opens his palms; the boy's quick to catch on
And opens his own palms and utters a sound—
He makes a pronouncement; it's clearly profound.

Yes, he's mastering language, each day more and muh
If he's after a drink, then he asks for 'wawar'.
He knows Mumma, Dadda, big sister's *'jeh jeh'*.
(He's multi-linguistic—that's the cute Chinese way!)

He's a regular twitcher[†]—for 'bird' he says, "Buh"
Most important of all he responds with a 'Ta'.
He's a cute little cupcake, that is for sure;
And oh Grandad loves it when he asks for 'muh'!

[†] serious bird watcher

The Book Lover

Big sister is reading and though he's just one,
He has books all around him; he thinks they are fun.
Yes, he likes nothing better than to stand by the shelf
And to pull every book out on top of himself!

Or if there are book sets that come in a box
Let's say Dr Seuss books (You know, *Fox in Sox*)
He likes nothing better than to take the books out
Then to put them back in—with a smidgen of help!

Or perhaps when the books are all out on the floor
And the box is quite empty, he likes nothing more
Than to act like a cat and to try to climb in
All the while, like the Cheshire cat, with a big grin!

Yes indeed, books are fun, but don't be deceived;
With books all around him, he is learning to read
And although he spreads books all around in a muddle,
He'll pick out a favourite and sit down for a cuddle.

And as he leans back in the crook of your arm
You think he at last has succumbed to the charm
Of reading a story; but, no, our young man
Loves to turn all the pages just as fast as he can!

He knows that for stories the pages must turn
It is one of those things that he's trying to learn.
His fine motor skills are developing fast
But the edges of pages are quite hard to grasp.

And what matters now is that pictures are fun:
A cat on a sofa, a dog on the run,
Especially when there is something to feel
Like a fluffy white tail or a cold metal wheel.

And if Grandma starts singing, as Grandmothers do,
A song with a star in it (or banana or two)
He'll head for the book pile and pick out the book
And 'twinkle' his fingers with a starry-eyed look.

He'll point to a star, very proud of himself
That he can pronounce it, the smart little elf.
The power of language has Big Sis in its grasp
And her book loving brother is joining her fast.

The Entertainer

He lifts up his shirt and he pats on his tummy;
He's one and a half and he thinks it is funny.
And then he is off down the hall with a skip
Sideways like a crab at a rather fast clip!

But should he trip over a rug or a broom,
He isn't a wimp; instead he chimes, "Bmmm";
And 'Bmmm' he calls out if he hears a door bang
Or a truck is off-loaded nearby with a clang.

Now swatting a fly is a bundle of fun.
He's seen Daddy do it; he knows how it's done!
He picks up the fly swat and runs 'round the room
Swatting at flies calling 'Bmmm', 'Bmmm' and 'Bmmm'!

His next entertainment is to press the remote.
If the TV should turn on, oh boy does he gloat!
And then the remote has turned into a phone
He is talking in prattle—he's seen how it's done!

But if he stands still with an air of mystique,
His forefinger poised on his left or right cheek
You know he's heard something—just follow his eyes:
It could be a bird or a jet in the skies;

It could be a truck or perhaps the postman
Or there in the driveway, a delivery van.
It could be a knocking out at the front door
His hearing's acute; it's wise not to ignore.

And once that is sorted, he heads off with a skip—
He's noticed my laptop in its bag with a zip.
And zippers are fun—if you get them to move.
He looks up and nods; I nod back to approve.

Yes, little man, you can give it a go—
Life should be fun, not just no, no and no!
My notebook is in there; you know your reward…
And when the zip moves, he knows that he's scored!

So out comes the notebook; he hands it to me.
I sit at the table; he climbs up on my knee.
While his program is loading and he waits for his thrill,
This born entertainer is finally still!

Grandparents' Day

In the back of the car, our little Prep girl
Is singing her heart out as we head off to school.
It's a song learnt in chapel: how love is the way.
Her little heart's happy as it's Grandparents' Day.

And then she decides to come up with a rhyme—
A game often played in the car to pass time.
Sometimes they are serious; often they're funny:
So 'funny' and 'sunny' or 'ning nong ninny nunny'!

At school, preppies gather together in class.
We are made to feel welcome; assembly is first,
With a welcome to country a matter of course,
And stories and speeches with songs interspersed.

There is one little story of a butterfly's struggle:
It finds to escape its cocoon is a tussle,
Which is needed to give its pretty wings muscle!
"Overcome to become" is the head-master's parable.

And then it is time for a feast morning tea,
Grandparents enjoying how every preppie
Hoes into a sandwich, some fruit or a cake:
They are having a great time, make no mistake!

After that it is time for a 'romp in the forest':
There are fun things to do—we are given a big list.
There are physical challenges and also a maze
And sliming one's hands is a popular craze.

All the tasks have a purpose: to make preppies think
Perhaps do some research; and they're tickled pink
That parked in the forest for them to hop in
Is a Queensland police car, its loud siren wailing!

But the art room provides a quieter challenge:
A mosaic-type task with glass bits to arrange
On a word on a board as best they are able.
The preppie can choose any word on the table.

The child finds a word that she thinks best describes
Her grandparents—friendly, loving, or kind
Or cuddly or fond or caring or smiling—
The children enjoy the task of selecting.

And grandparents watch with interest to learn
How they are perceived by their own special one
For little ones often are very percipient!
And our little preppie picks up the word 'patient'.

And then she proceeds to engage in the task
With shard upon shard of the colourful glass
Placed in position; Grandma pastes the glue,
While our preppie persists and sees the task through.

Patience indeed! Now that that task is done
It's time to go outdoors and join everyone;
But of all of the things done on Grandparents' Day,
I think most of how patient is our Amber Mei.

The Drive

As we're driving along, in the back of the car
Our little one's chanting the small repertoire
Of words he can say. He is just having fun,
This cute little fellow, this son of a gun.

We've just passed some roadworks; he's seen a big 'digger',
A word that he knows, so that's been the trigger.
It's as if he has had a sudden epiphany:
The light has snapped on to reveal a great mystery.

And, as everyone knows, for many a boy,
A digger is truly their favourite toy.
Especially when, as for this little fellow,
It is painted his favourite colour, bright yellow!

And so in the back, he delights to the sound
Of his voice forming words, and the knowledge profound
That these sounds are a way to make sense of the world
The power of language is being unfurled.

It's hard not to smile when he calls out 'hello'.
He recites many colours; his favourite's 'lellow'.
He says it with awe and the same's true of 'porple'
And similar words such as 'bubble' and 'tortle'!

He knows 'sun' and 'moon' though his favourite's 'star'.
When there's rain on the windscreen, he calls out 'ra ra'.
His 'No' is emphatic, but honest to God,
His yes breaks one up: it's a vigorous nod!

He is quite an enthusiast; calling out 'yay' and 'wow'
And 'moo' is the sound that is made by a cow.
And if there's a loud noise, of course it is 'boom';
And a 'door' must be opened to enter a room.

When cutting his playdough, he calls out 'cut, cut';
Or he'll run around naked and call out 'butt, butt'.
And his soft little bunny is known as 'bun, bun'
While his little cars rev to the sound of 'brmm, brmm'!

But his favourite words as we cruise in the car
Are the words for his family, words like 'Dadda';
And the name of his mother he says with a hum:
He holds on to the end as he says the word, "Mummm".

He has a good go at 'Grandma' and 'Grandpa'
Then suddenly breaks into 'la! la! la! la!'
Which is something his sister has taught him to say,
And when saying her name, he calls her, "Jeh jeh".

As we're driving along, we listen enchanted:
He's reciting his words and we have been granted
An insight into how a young mind is growing
His language has started and soon will be flowing.

As we're driving along, in the back of the car,
There's suddenly silence: the best sound by far
When the point of the drive is to get him to sleep;
We both give a smile and a sigh of relief.

Yes, the young man is sleeping, perhaps in his dreams
A sense of excitement is shaping his memes.
But Grandma and Grandad drive on in a glow
Having witnessed his joyful vocabulary show!

Dan Dan Do!

Little Mister Independent likes to have a go
And so, in no uncertain terms, he clearly lets us know
(No matter that he's biting off more than a tyke can chew!)
That he would like to take control; he tells us, "Dan Dan do!"

Yes, Dan Dan now is two years old as of a week ago.
He's putting words together—soon the sentences will flow.
"Sit down," he says and pats the lounge so one must take a
       pew:
Well, that was his first sentence; so, of sorts, is, "Dan Dan do!"

We've put the stroller up so we can take him for a walk
But before we've reached the turn into the Happy Valley
       Boardwalk
The little man wants out of there; he'd like to push his bear.
He cannot reach the handles so the stroller's hard to steer.

Now the purpose of the outing varies with your point of view
But for little Dan, it's very much a case of Dan Dan do!
Though the stroller has a tendency to prop and swerve and
       veer,
We let him push but help him steer if anyone is near!

At dinner time, he's mastering his little spoon and fork
He's quite determined he will spear that little bit of pork.
No matter that the spoon is upside down, the fork is skew;
Don't try to lend a hand or you'll be scolded 'Dan Dan do!'

We're sitting at my notebook waiting for a site to load,
A site with little diggers having fun building a road.
He knows to start it working there are steps one must go
        through:
I tell him 'Click', he gives a grin and prattles, "Dan Dan do!"

Oh many are the tasks the little man would love to master
And so long as it's not dangerous, not heading for disaster
It's fun to watch the lad persist, to 'paddle his own canoe';
And we love to watch and marvel at the power of Dan Dan do!

The Graduate

High up in the air all the mortar boards are twirling:
It's graduation day so it's time for celebrating.
Great things have been achieved this year, but this we can't
      ignore:
The candidates are kindy kids and most of them are four!

They each have a certificate and speeches have been made
And each has walked across the floor, a little promenade:
A tiny little ritual to show them how it's done;
A nervous little moment but a moment in the sun!

Proud parents watch with grinning pride their little son or
      daughter,
Hoping all the while that their darling does not falter.
And then it's time to photograph the class of '17
And judge it as the smartest class that they have ever seen!

Such ceremonies mark for us life's little rites of passage
And on occasions such as these, I think upon the adage:
Children are the messages…to a time we will not see.
What message will these children take into posterity?

But what they know for now is just that they are celebrating
And yummy cupcakes have been made which now require
        devouring!
And Mum and Dad, Grandma, Grandpa rejoice with Amber
        Mei
On this, her first experience of a graduation day.

The Teacher

"Daniel," she says, "let's count."

Counting is fun, especially for a two-year-old
with a big sister to lead the way.

She does the odd numbers, he the evens:
One TWO three FOUR five SIX seven EIGHT nine TEN.
What enthusiasm for numbers
as he SHOUTS them at the top of his voice!

"Daniel," she says, "let's sing."

Singing is fun, especially when it is done in chorus
with a big sister to provide the continuo!

"…and on that farm he has a cow."
MOO MOO he sings at the top of his voice
What enthusiasm for music
as he sings at the top of his voice!

"Daniel," she says, "let's play I Spy."

I Spy is fun when big sister plays it with colours:
"I spy something that's yellow," she says.
(A judge might call that a leading question!)

"YELLOW DIGGER!" he answers.
What enthusiasm for colours as he
SHOUTS them at the top of his voice!

"Daniel," she says, "would you like a story?"

Reading is fun, especially when Big Sister knows
That your favourite story at the moment is…

"The GRUFFALO" he shouts as she points to the words.
What enthusiasm for reading
as he points to the pictures…
but sometimes he imitates her and points to the words too.
No matter that he is pointing in the wrong place!
He is getting the idea.

And very soon his brain will make the connections
and he will be reading on his own
Just as she now is.

What a teacher!

Mummy! Mummy!

There's blood on his mouth and blood on his finger:
Where has it come from, we ponder and wonder!
He was happy as happy a moment ago
But all of a sudden, he's stricken with woe.

All day he has played with his new tip-up truck
And new yellow digger—they're presents from Luke,
The landscaper building two solid rock walls
With digger and dumpy; and Dan's been enthralled.

Dan's vocab's increasing and now it includes
'Digger' and 'Luke' as two popular words.
When Luke kindly lifted him up on the digger,
The smile on his face just grew bigger and bigger.

His big sister too was given a turn
And she took great pleasure in blowing the horn—
Wonderful medicine, one has to say,
For a preppie not well and kept home for the day!

Well, the walls are both finished, but to Dan Dan's surprise
Luke came by this morning with two packaged toys
The digger and truck, as aforesaid, both yellow.
A source of delight for wide-eyed little fellow!

So he played with the digger while he sat in the truck,
Which is just wide enough for his be-nappied butt!
Then he tipped up the tip truck to tip out the 'rocks',
A cute little pile of bundled up socks!

But tonight, his attention had turned to the box
That the digger was packed in—and here came the shock:
When the cardboard collapsed as he pushed on the lid,
He fell in with a fright, the poor little kid.

There's blood on his mouth and blood on his finger:
Where has it come from we ponder and wonder!
Our faces crowd 'round all full of concern
But there's no major damage that we can discern.

He was happy as happy a moment ago
But all of a sudden, he's stricken with woe.
And in his distress, he calls, "Mummy! Mummy!"
Sis hands him his 'Bear Bear' to clutch to his tummy.

In confused consternation, he calls out, "Dan Dan"—
He has had quite a fright has our dear little man;
But his mummy's warm hug and her voice will subdue
His fright and his sobbing and he'll quickly pull through.

He isn't a wimp; no, he's not one to cry
Whenever there's upset and things go awry;
But this was unnerving, a bolt from the blue…
And in cases like this, only Mummy will do!

68

The Lesson 1

Grandma's in the water with her little grandson;
He is learning to swim and having great fun.
The teacher is singing and splashing her hands
So he splashes with gusto; his wide grin expands.

Climbing onto the mat as it floats on the water,
He toddles across it when some others falter.
Grandma is waiting so he takes a big leap
And kicking his legs he bursts up from the deep.

He is learning to float: as he lies on his back,
His head on her shoulder, he starts to relax
And looks up in the mirror the teacher is holding
For keeping his head back ensures he keeps floating.

At the edge of the pool, he climbs up on the wall
Teacher sings, "Humpty Dumpty" and then they all fall
And here they are learning to turn themselves 'round
And head for the railing so they won't be drowned.

On the side of the pool perched on grandfather's knee,
His big sister comments with visible glee
On the way that her brother is learning to swim
And it's clear that she's really delighted for him.

The lesson is over, he's starting to cry
For he says he is cold, but soon he is dry.
He toddles across to the centre café,
Where he knows he will get a reward for the day.

The Lesson 2

The ginger-bread man didn't stand a chance
I knew he was for it from the very first glance
From our two-year-old grandson, who of course had caught
    sight
Of the bright smartie buttons; it was love at first bite!

There was never a question of what would go first:
Those bright coloured smarties all disappeared fast
And then he decided to chomp off an arm
But the ginger-bread man had lost none of his charm.

He still had his head, there were three limbs to go;
The only decision was what to eat now!
Such decisions of course must be carefully weighed…
Then all of a sudden it was 'off with his head'!

Pretty soon what was left was a lonely torso
But by now the hot pace was beginning to slow;
And besides, the attention of this little rascal
Had changed: he had spotted the big bouncing castle!

So he slipped from my knee and was off at a pace.
Big sister and Grandad got up and gave chase
And brother and sister bounced on, on and on
Cementing in laughter their familial bond.

We are on the way home, we put on a CD,
Some nursery rhymes and the odd lullaby,
And soon silence emanates from the back seat
The morning's exertions have put them to sleep!

Dan Dan and the Dumpy

Daddy has borrowed a dumpy,
A motorised barrow on tracks.
It can carry fourfold
What a push barrow holds
But the load doesn't break Daddy's back!

The dumpy has levers that drive it;
They make it go forwards and back.
They lift up the bucket
And tip out what's in it
And my daddy's acquired the knack!

When Daddy is using the dumpy,
Sometimes he will give us a ride.
Despite all the racket,
We sit in the bucket
And wave to the adults outside.

The dumpy is stored in the garage;
I love to go out there to play.

On the back, legs astride,
I stand up there with pride
'Cos I wanna be like Daddy one day!

I point to the switch on the engine,
Shake my head side to side, say, "No! No!"
But inside me I yearn
To give it a turn:
How I wish I could make dumpy go!

And then there's a rope with a handle;
How I'd relish to give that a pull!
Though I've seen Daddy do it
My muscles aren't up to it
But just holding it gives me a thrill!

Daddy has borrowed a dumpy
And while I have plenty of toys
I just have to say
When it comes down to play,
I like toys that are made for big boys!

Sleeping Beauty

Children sing in minor thirds
(As in fact do many birds)
When they play, kids love the sound
Of tunes like 'Seesaw up and down'!

So when teaching Amber Mei
At the piano, how to play,
Grandma gets her first to sing
Little rhymes that Grandad brings;
High note   then the
    first and   low
Learning   rhythms
    how the   go.
On the keys, two coloured stickers
Show her where to put her fingers.
Just a minor third apart,
This is where the lessons start!

As repetition is the key,
Grandad soon found out that he
Had the task of writing rhymes
About her world at various times!

Thus, a trip to 'Sleeping Beauty'
Led to this brief rhythmic summary
(All done in the line of duty!)

The king and queen have had a daughter;
She is called Princess Aurora.

Carabosse, the evil fairy,
Puts a spell on the young baby.

Lilac Fairy interferes—
Aurora sleeps one hundred years!

Lilac fairy tells a prince,
Who wakes Aurora with a kiss.

The Prince and Sleeping Beauty marry.
Everyone is very happy!

Rhythms pulsate in my dreams.
As do minor harmonies.
Hope it's time to move on soon
To when we sing a *major* tune!

The Tale of Little Fellow

While some soft toys are rather large, some cuddle toys are
    small
And there's no knowing which soft toy will hold within its
    thrall
A little child, or which soft toy will be their special friend,
A presence that will comfort them, on whom they can
    depend.

Big Moosie lives in Grandad's car between two booster seats
And with him Little Moosie waits to greet our little guests;
And many are the times a child's succumbed to Moosie
    charms
And nodded off to sleep with a soft Moosie in their arms.

But there is yet another friend for whom the car is home:
A skinny little mouse that has a long and pointy nose.
His torso fits quite snuggly within a child's small palm
While little hands can grasp with ease a gangly leg or arm.

He's joined the car menagerie; he's really quiet at home
Perched over a side window in the clothes hook, looking
        down
Or peeking 'round the headrest at the back of Grandma's seat
Or dancing to some music as a child moves to the beat!

Now given that this mouse's crew are Big and Little Moosie
You wouldn't be surprised if he'd acquired the title Mousie!
But no, that's not the way of it; he got his name by chance
And how he got his moniker came down to circumstance.

Our little grand-daughter was two and really not herself—
One of those days a child becomes a fractious little elf—
When Grandma reached deep down into her Mary Poppins
        bag
And in her hand, when it came out, she held this gangly wag.

And turning to our grand-daughter, who looked a little sallow,
She asked her if she'd like a cuddle from 'this little fellow'.
The little fellow did the trick and quickly cheered her up
And very soon she nodded off with new friend on her lap.

The next time she was with us in the back of Grandad's auto
She asked us what had happened to her new friend 'Little
        Fellow'.
When she looked up, to her surprise, he was above her
        window
Held there by the handle/hook, exuding mouse machismo.

So 'Little Fellow' is his name and now a few years on
Our grandson likes to hold him and to have a conversation
And Big and Little Moosie do not seem to mind a bit
That Little Fellow (bless him!) has become the children's
        favourite.

79

Mr Cranky Pants

Hey! Hey! Mr Cranky Pants! What's this all about?
No need to be so fractious. No need for you to pout.
You've missed out on your day sleep; your world is out of joint
For lack of sleep has pushed you way beyond your tipping
point!

Where's Mummy's little Munchkin? Where can the rascal be?
I'm sure he's 'round here somewhere; let's have a look and see!
Where's Grandma's ragamuffin? Where's Daddy's little scamp?
Where's Grandad's charming scallywag? Let's find the little imp!

Has he gone into hiding? Is he underneath the table?
Maybe he's just floated off inside a magic bubble!
Maybe he's on holiday with bunny, bear and ted;
Perhaps he's turned invisible and standing on his head!

Hey! Hey! Mr Cranky Pants! Watch out here comes a spider
He's creeping up your arm and soon will run over your
shoulder
Look out for his long finger legs—I think he means to tickle
Oh no! He's changing course and heading headlong for your
middle!

Hey! Hey! Little Munchkin! What's that I hear—a chuckle?
That spider sure knows what to do to make a munchkin
      giggle!
Well, Grandma, would you look at this; we have our munchkin
      back.
Young Cranky Pants has left the room—and munchkin needs
      a snack!

I Being Careful

He's growing up fast; he's a boy in a hurry!
With his physical prowess, he lives life adventurously,
But we'd sometimes prefer that he lived life less zealously!
From up on a wall, where he's balanced precariously,
He says to his grandad, who's watching him nervously,
"I be careful, Grandad; don't you worry!"

Big sister has learnt how to ride her two-wheeler;
His balance bike's fun and he try to keep up with her.
"Slow down!" Grandma calls as she senses disaster.
But he calls as he tries to go faster and faster,
(Not realising he still has a few skills to master!)
"I be careful, Grandma; don't you worry!"

Tree branches are made for a young boy to climb
And he's found one that temptingly bends to the ground.
It looks like a fun seat, it looks safe and sound.
So he says as we help him up onto the limb,
Not keen at the way our hands navigate him:
"I'm okay now…I careful…don't worry."

There are plenty of things to climb on in the park
And he thinks that the climbing wall there is a lark
And while he accepts that we help at the start,
Guiding a foot when it's wide of the mark,
As he shimmies up foot- and hand-holds he remarks,
"I'm okay now…I careful…don't worry."

Well it's good to have courage, it's good to have skills
And it is nice you enjoy all these physical thrills
As long as they don't end in too many spills!
So let us protect you while you have your fill
For our caution is just what experience instils:
Please forgive us; we're just being careful!

Carbon-Based Bipeds

It's quite a thick book, collected essays by Arthur C. Clarke,
A tome befitting the prophet of the Space Age:

Greetings, Carbon-Based Bipeds!

"Your book is boring" is the judgement of
   our four-year-old grand-son.
"Well, I know there aren't any pictures…
   but there are a lot of interesting words!"
"You know, your book must be a chatterbox, Grandad!"
"You know, I think you are right, Dan Dan.
A chatterbox certainly uses a lot of words!
And this book is a very *interesting* chatterbox!"

He picks up my bookmark, and places it on the page.
"There you go," he says, closing the book.
He grabs my hand and pulls me to my feet.
Gym is over and it is time to go home.
I carry him over the rough stones in the car park.
He knows which button to press on the remote
(and how to press my buttons!)

I open his door, he climbs in; but his booster seat
is far less interesting than the driver's seat!
Climbing into the front, he perches with his hands
Firmly on the steering wheel. Querulously:
"When will I be old enough to drive, Grandad?"
"In just a few years, Dan, Dan."
With excitement: "When I'm eleventeen."
"Indeed! When you're eleventeen!"

But Grandma knows how to press his buttons…
and the visual temptation of a snack on his booster seat
severs the yearning that tethers him to the steering wheel!
Window down as we leave the gym grounds, he looks for
the donkey and miniature horse in the paddock opposite—
a weekly ritual! Snack over, warning sounds emanate
from the back seat: "Octopod in danger! Oooh! Oooh! Oooh!"
Dashi, Peso and Captain Barnacle are at home
So koala has come to the rescue. Suddenly, silence—and then:
"You know, Grandad, this koala is brown; he should be grey!
Koalas are grey, Grandad. True fact!"
"Well spotted, Dan. Maybe he dyed his fur for fun!"

At home, Grandma and Dan Dan nestle down,
She on her e-pad and he on his iPad…
but before long, the iPad needs charging!
"Look, Grandma. Zero percent!" He knows that
that means that the battery has run out of energy.
"Let's go for a walk and post your letter to aunty Linda
while the iPad is recharging." So Grandma and Dan Dan
go for a long walk to the letterbox.

He is a great walker,
but the steep driveway at the end of the walk is too much.
He lies down on the grass and declares:
"Zero percent! Carry me!"
One little carbon-based biped has had a big day!

Little Legs

"Do you like my new suit?" he asks random wedding guests.
"Oh, yes. You look very smart, young man."
They grin at the artlessness of a three-year-old.
Openness, innocence, cuteness wrapped in a ball of
anticipation and excitement.
We're at a wedding and he knows that this is somehow
      special…
After all, he has been decked out in a smart blue jacket
and his little legs in new long blue trousers!

It is very much a family affair and little legs there are aplenty,
running hither and thither on the inviting open lawns of the
      winery.
Parents hope that some of the energy will dissipate
before the open-air ceremony begins.
Stern instructions are issued…and all is going well;
but while a wedding ceremony is all very well for a while,
skill acquisition is central to a three-year-old's world view:
Snort! Snort! Comes from along the row.
He has just remembered that recently he discovered
how to snort like a pig! Big legs move quickly
to remove the clear and present danger!

Then there are petals to throw—and once thrown,
to be gathered from the lawn and thrown again…
but this time not at the bride and groom!
Little legs, released from the bondage of inactivity,
just want to run…to kick the soccer ball with new friends:
Harrison becomes his buddy for the afternoon.

Little legs dangle on a garden wall: snack time to recharge
        little legs!
And then, like elastic bungee cords stretching and recoiling,
Little legs radiate away from adults and then return,
Gradually with less frequency as certainty of security is
        assured.

At dusk, in the pavilion, there is much wide-eyed pointing
as little legs gather around a table of wedding cakes!
At the table, new suit and his new buddy spy bread rolls –
and bread rolls mean BUTTER! Finger licking good!
Food fit for a wedding feast and of much more interest
than mountain salmon, pork belly or Otago lamb shoulder!

Out in the barn, when it is time to Strip the Willow,
little legs in a suit have finally grown tired,
happy to collapse into a welcoming and capacious bean bag
and succumb to the hypnotising rhythms of Céilí jigs and
        reels.

…but out on the dance floor other little legs are jigging:
Six-year-old big sister is caught up in the palpable joy of the
        occasion
And cousin Kai, slightly older, shares her enthusiasm for the

dance.
Now fathers swirl with little-legs daughters, mothers with
        little-legs sons,
cousins with cousins, new friends with new little-legs friends!
They form an arch…and high-heeled adults aglow bend low
accommodating the joy of little legs and low arches.

Enthralled by the Céilí band, big sister and Kai draw up
        chairs
to sit, stare and savour the effusive joy of the musicians
before leaping up to join in another reel.
On a bean bag in the corner, other little legs have finally
        collapsed,
some on top of their dozing daddies!
But four little legs dance on till the adults drop and the music
        stops.
And then, little-legged *joie de vivre* proclaims the undeniable
        truth:
        "This was the best wedding ever!"

Kids' Time

Kids run on kids' time; their setting is slow!
Just you try to hurry them when it's time to go!
It's often been said, as all parents will know:
"We should have been gone fifteen minutes ago!"

The clock may be ticking; you should be away.
But the game is a good one, they'd much rather stay;
And many a parent has been heard to say:
"Come on now, you munchkins; we don't have all day!"

While adults are conscious they're going to be late!
A kid likes to dawdle, to procrastinate;
I'm sure you have heard a fraught parent berate:
"How much longer, you kids, do we all have to wait?"

But once in the car, it's a pretty sure bet
That time's passing too slowly and kids start to fret.
Soon querulous voices will ask: "…we there yet?"
To which the unfortunate response is a 'Nyet!'

Birthday parties are fun but when it comes to the day,
An afternoon party seems far, far away!
The clock ticks too slowly; they don't like delay.
How they wish that the party would get under way!

Or if Santa is coming, it's too long to wait!
Excitement is brewing so, not to tempt fate,
They go to bed early, they don't stay up late;
Such is their excitement, they'll be early awake!

Kids run on kids' time; sometimes it is slow
But then other times it is all systems go!
That time is quite relative physicists know;
But so too do parents watching little kids grow!

In the Whole Wide World

"Did you know," he says, "the conoconut cwab
is the biggest cwab *in the whole wide world*?"
In the front of the car, Grandma and Grandad are grinning
      inwardly;
but, in the back, big sister can't help herself!
"Which cwab?" she giggles cheekily.
"You know! The conoconut cwab! It's the biggest cwab
in the whole wide world."
"Oh, you mean the coconut crab!"
"Yes, the conoconut cwab! It's the biggest."

His appetite for facts about the natural world is insatiable.
In the library, he chooses his own books:
Dinosaurs, sharks, reptiles…critters of all kinds.

We learn from him that the chimp
is the smartest land animal
in the whole wide world

that the bottlenose dolphin
is the smartest sea critter
in the whole wide world

that the cheetah
is the fastest land animal
in the whole wide world

that the peregrine falcon
is the fastest bird
in the whole wide world

Don't be deceived. Although he's just four
and some words are difficult to get a little tongue around
his hunger for knowledge has led to
the rapid acquisition of reading skills…
(aided greatly by having big sister as his wingman!)

And to Grandma and me,
our *wonder-full* grandson
is the cutest little munchkin
in the whole wide world!

The Muse

There's no knowing when the muse will tap one on the
      shoulder;
No knowing when she will seduce one into activity:
A word, a phrase, an existential moment of sparkling anxiety
(Clearly not to be mixed up with the existentialism region in
      France!)
Demanding to be bottled and preserved for future delectation,
What oft was thought but ne'er so well expressed!
Something to make you, them say, "Ah yes, that's how it is…"
Words bubbling with effervescent clarity, freshness, essence!
Heaven forbid that they should fizz into a tale told by an idiot
      Signifying nothing!
But when a grandson, grinning, wearing his daddy's shades,
Comes running into the room calling, "Look me! Look me!"
Now that really is something; that demands attention!
Oh, Lord, look at him! LOOK at him!

A Dung Cart Full of Kisses

Celebrating
Family and Friends

Fuzzy Pictures

Swallows are difficult critters to photograph!
They dart and weave—no time to
get them in the field of view
let alone focus!
They must have amazing eyesight
because in mid-flight, for one millisecond,
they can swerve and hover to peck an insect out of the air.
There's your chance!
Fat chance!

But I do have one photo
where the insect is almost in focus
but
dammit
the swallow's face is fuzzy!
What a shot it WOULD have been!
Not even Photoshop can fix that one!
Near miss!
If only!

We are in Merthyr looking for Dad's childhood home
but the signage is confusing
so we stop to ask two ladies chatting
at the front door of a home that
we THINK is in Queen's Road,
explaining: *from Australia…in search of our roots.*
They, courteous, interested, responding:
Grandma is 95 but as sharp as a tack.
She will remember; come in for a cuppa;
but sharp-as-a-tack Grandma says there were
definitely NO Garretts in Queen's Road.

A few years later, discovery, epiphany!
Discovery: Great Grandad was George –
George, as in *George Frederick Handel* Garrett:
Greater love hath no man for a composer
than he gives the full moniker to his son!
Oh, we had seen photos of the family orchestra,
George's family orchestra!

Discovery: Grandad's wedding certificate:
Fred Garrett, also known professionally as Fred Handel

Epiphany: They were professional—
and used a stage name:
The *Handel* Family Orchestra.
No wonder I had not found them in the
1891 census.
Bingo! Handels—all listed as musicians!
Even in 1891, marketing was everything!

So sharp-as-a-tack Grandma was right:
There were no Garretts in Queen's Road
only Handels!
If only we had known what we know now,
what might she have remembered?

If only!

Discovery: Postcards addressed to Ernie *Handel*!
Dad grew up as a Handel.
But Dad was taciturn; never talked about his past.
Wished he had;
we would have had a sharper picture.
If only!

Falling into Step

I bought a kit through Ancestry to check my DNA,
Which found my link with cousin Dot, who's half a world
away.
Our grand-parents were siblings, although fourteen years the
gap,
And Dot and I through emails have now fallen into step.

The search for family history is of course a common bond
But it seems that there are other things of which we both are
fond
So it's not surprising that we chat on every other day
For in this modern world, she's just an internet away.

She's a member of a sewing group; it's something of a
passion
For the ladies making dresses for *A Stitch in Time* at
Wellington.
She meets with friends, they chew the fat and in no time at all
They've made a dozen dresses for poor children in Nepal.

Dot had an elder sibling, a Big Brother, her BB,
Who turned his hand to painting and to writing poetry
And though BB had cancer and has, sadly, passed away
I feel that I have known him through a common artistry.

And even though his great grandson has only just been born
Through this new leaf upon the tree, his legacy lives on.
And while I bring Dot up to date on new leaves in Australia,
She shares with me the latest news on little Alexander.

My wife and I have driven south to visit long-time friends
Whose friendship dates back decades—a friendship that
        transcends
The vagaries of time and space…so whenever we meet up
We find from our first greeting that we've fallen into step.

Some things are serendipitous, some things seem meant to be
But it really seems quite natural for cousin Dot and me
That we should seem like long-time friends whose history
        goes back
And there's nothing quite like friendships where one falls
        right into step.

Steering True

My mate Frank is an affable bloke:
He likes to chat and he likes to joke;
And down at the men's shed with his mates
He works at fixing bicycle brakes.

And if the chain is hanging too loosely
They fix the tension so gears change smoothly.
They also ensure that the steering is true
So a second-hand bike is as good as new!

They package the bikes in a shipping container
And send them off to new homes in Africa
Where the bikes are the source of effulgent joy
For many young girls and for many a boy.

And overseas in Shropshire, England,
Making nice clothes for poor African children,
Cousin Dot is making some frocks
For an organisation called 'Love in a Box'!

And while each frock has its own design,
Each frock must have one feature divine:
And that is a pocket, because that is where
They insert a freshly-made cute teddy bear!

Now Frank and Dot live a world apart
But down in the depths of my beating heart
I wonder if somewhere in deepest Uganda
A thrilled little girl rides a bike in a pinafore.

And in her pocket maybe is a teddy
And her bike steers true and her gears change smoothly.
Now Frank is an atheist; Dot is devout
But they both seem to know what life's really about!

A Dung Cart Full of Kisses

In my grandma's photo album, which has been bequeathed
    to me
Is this postcard from her brother and from other family:
Alf and Frank both send their love to you, my sister dear,
And a dung cart full of kisses to last you through the year.

Well, Grandma's folk were farmers, but that I did not know
Until my parents passed away some fourteen years ago.
It was then I started wondering what my heritage might be
So I set about researching and commenced a family tree.

The photo album gave some clues, her birthday book gave
    more
And added to the little bit I knew from family lore;
I looked on familysearch.org for baptisms and births
And also joined ancestry.com to see what that was worth.

Births, marriages and deaths are there from 1837,
When Britain started centralising civil registration.
Prior to that, one has to know which parish folk were in
And search those parish records if you wish to find your kin.

The records are transcriptions done by willing volunteers,
Who try to read the hand-writing but errors do appear;
And should one be so lucky as to search on the right track,
A look at the originals will help pick up mistakes.

And census records too are there from eighteen forty-one;
And every decade after that a census has been done.
However, the last one hundred years are under lock and key
In order to respect the living and their privacy.

My great-great-grandfather was James; I knew his wife was
    Mary
Baptismal records were a clue to guess when they were married:
The first child to be christened was in eighteen twenty-five
So I guessed the marriage happened just before baby arrived.

No record could I find of it; but thinking laterally
I searched newspaper archives around the year that it should be.
Imagine my delight at finding in the *Worcester Journal*
The announcement of the marriage there in satisfying detail!

Wills and gravestones also helped trace family history
(Helpful too, I have to say, was serendipity!)
And finally I bought a kit and sent a vial away
To see what family history lies within my DNA!

And so it is that looking back to trace my pedigree
Has linked me up with living cousins searching just like me!
That's just one reason why it is on research I'm so hooked;
You don't know who or what you'll find until you've really
    looked.

There are cousins in Australia; it's here that I call home.
There are cousins in the UK, from whence my family comes.
Two cousins are in Canada and so it is, you see,
Between us all we're building up a mighty family tree.

Some forebears were musicians, who played professionally,
Sometimes they played on cruise ships as they cruised about
        the sea.
One was a station master; one was a factor's clerk.
And some of them were sailors or did stevedoring work.

We have forebears who were farmers, from Templecombe to
        Lea;
While some of them were linmen, whatever that might be!
And more than one girl left her home to be a governess,
While some lived in an orphanage, including Grandma Bess.

So who were Alf and Frank who sent their love so long ago
To Grandma Bess? Through years of research, I can say I
        know!
Indeed, by tracing all grand-parents and their pedigrees
I have a working knowledge dating back four centuries.

And so I wish to send you through the medium of rhyme,
Wherever you are sited in the realms of space and time,
A dung cart full of kisses, my cousins everyone.
Who knows where this our search will lead? Perhaps it's just
        begun!

Christmas Greetings

Would you like to have a coffee? Would you like to have a
    chat
And bring me up to date about your life and where you're at?
I hope that you've found happiness though life can be unkind
So I'd love to have a coffee—find out what is on your mind.

Would you like to have a drink with me, perhaps a Christmas
    beer
To celebrate our friendship and to spread some Christmas
    cheer?
The world is full of drama; there is much our hearts lament
But let's drink to our long friendship and the good times we
    have spent.

Would you like to walk the boardwalk; 'twould be nice to
    take a stroll
Recalling happy memories and, should you wish to bare your
    soul,
Then that's okay with me, my friend, 'cos that's what friends
    are for
Especially with a friendship stretching back to days of yore.

We only see each other now just once or twice a year
But in no way does that imply our friendship's not sincere;
Life's busy-ness intrudes so we must do what we must do
But, my friend, at Christmas time I always think of you.

Would you like to have a coffee? Is there time to have a
      beer?
No matter if there isn't time—it's a busy time of year.
So just in case there isn't time, well I'd just like to say:
I wish you joy and peace and love, my friend, this Christmas
      Day.

On Location

Reflecting on Experiences
in
Particular Places

Japan:
Haiku

With blossoms now, the garden is ablaze
But this one perfect blossom holds my gaze.

Melbourne Park Tennis Centre: Lanky Legs

The Summer of Women's Tennis in Australia
is a season of lanky legs!
Ladies and gentlemen, please welcome to centre court
the iskovas and uskovas, the ovas and povas;
the enkas and emskas, the inas and linas
and other fine-legged fillies from the steppes of Eurasia!

Ears pricked, alert and focused at the barrier,
they jig a little jig during the toss,
impatient for the starter's gun; and then,
with the Nike goddess of Victory perched on their shoulders,
they race to their end of the court to 'just do it':
Swoosh! Swoosh!

Legs full of running have been trained for this:
double-handed backhand to double-handed backhand;
double-handed forehand to double-handed forehand!
Moving forward to the baseline,
lanky legs bend low to meet the trajectory of the ball
knees almost scraping the ground.

The return is short and the side-line is open.
Here's your chance: no guts, no glory!
With a whinny of climactic exertion, she punches down the line;
…but there's a fine side-line between pleasure and pain
and an omniscient hawk-eye god sits above,
ready to stand in judgement!

Straight of back, long of limb, the goddesses of tennis
battle to the *oohs* and the *aahs* of the appreciative crowd.
But beware, all you tennis-morphic lanky-legged goddesses!
A five and a half foot happy little Aussie Vegemite from
team Jaguar is on the prowl.
With her Head racquet and her cheeky backhand slice,
she plans to bring you to your knees!

Flushing Meadows:
The Champion

Serena is a champion (Oh, yeh!)
Such a great champion (Former number one)
She's won a lot of titles (Twenty-three majors)
But Margaret Court is still ahead of her by one.

Serena made the finals (U.S. Open)
Played against Naomi (Osaka from Japan)
An awesome young talent (She's only 20)
And the match just wasn't going as Serena had planned!

Patrick Mouratoglou (Coaches Serena)
Gave some hand signals (Strictly banned!)
Umpire Carlos saw him (Experienced umpire)
Penalised Serena but gets booed by her fans.

Naomi broke her service (Kept her focus)
Serena wasn't happy (Not going to plan!)
Smashed a new racquet (Frame all broken)
Copped another penalty—as rules demand!

Serena now was spewing (Apoplectic!)
Vented on the umpire (Attacked the man!)
Called him sexist thief (Clear abuse—verbal)
Her fans were all behind her chanting from the stands.

Penalised a whole game (Third violation)
Serena was in tears (Couldn't understand)
Poor little Serena (Queen Serena)
Had only self to blame as she had forced his hand!

Mark Knight drew a cartoon (Satirical cartoon)
Capturing the meltdown (Man oh man!)
Umpire asks Naomi (Poor Naomi)
Couldn't you just let her win; she's out of hand!

Cartoon does not flatter (Well, she's in meltdown!)
Mark is branded racist (Hits the fan!)
Outraged fans are venting (Twitter! Twitter! Twitter!)
Serina hides her head in racist, sexist sand!

BUT…Her coach confessed to coaching (Oh, yeh!)
Serina smashed her racquet (Oh, yeh!)
Then abused the umpire (Oh, yeh!)
This is something for which she should carry the can!

AND…Let's forget Serena (Oh, Yeh!)
Let's applaud Naomi (from Japan)
Gracious young champion (U.S. Open)
The trophy is now hers; applaud the change of hands!

Brisbane, Australia: Glenleighden

These old school walls have many a tale to tell:
Let them enfold us with history's heart-warming hug.
Listen! And hear the lilt of Irish voices to be sure.
The Doughty family, McCulloughs, O'Briens and Breddins—
Chattering to the chink of bridles and the squeak of leather
As they dismount and set their horses to graze in the horse
paddock.

Listen:
and you might just hear the chanting of the four-times table;
And, after lunch, hear how Horatio defended the bridge—
A game for boys to stop and play at the creek on the way
home;
And other stories from the Queensland Readers.

Listen! Here comes the postman, clip-clop;
He ties up his horse at the cork tree.
This is a receiving office and, this, for the schoolmaster,
Is a serious responsibility.
The letters are passed on like relay batons
to the children's saddle-bags.

Listen again! It is the weekend.
Do you hear the echoing pock of the tennis balls
being hit on the new ant-bed tennis court?
This is the social day. And if you listen hard,
You just might hear the sound of reels,
the click of heels on a Saturday night;
Or the whirr of the movie projector—Saturday night fever
As the first travelling picture show hits the district.

Lean in with the walls and listen hard.
In the distance is the slow, silent rising of the flood waters.
Can you hear it above the rattling chains of rain on the iron
roof?
The sugar flats are under and soon so will be the houses.
Quick! Open the doors to Colleen and Paddy
and the Garrigons and the Sweeneys.
This is a high place; the high place—this is our school.
This is our community centre and we are safe.

Argentina:
Enmeshed in Tango

What is…this rhythm…in my… subconscious mind?
Can't get… the rhythm…out of… my head!
I should… be sleeping…jetlag…defeating
But my…first tango night is winning…instead.

Enmeshed…in tango…fishnet…fandango,
My mind …keeps pulsing to its insis…tent beat.
Neat sync…opation…filled with…elation
Couples…enmeshed in tango-fencing…feet.

Intense…emotion…passion…compulsion;
Pausing…and darting forward… gliding…with ease
United…in rhythm…this man and woman…driven
Enmeshed in…tango; never want to…leave.

France:
Très Beau

I can see myself in a chateau
Champagne tippling and eating gâteau
Trying out my Franglais
On a French holiday.
Mon Dieu! Does it not sound *très beau?*!

An Operating Theatre: Colons Inside-Out

So you're an English teacher?
Our last patient was a Maths teacher!
Must be teachers' day for colonoscopies!
Just clench and pump your fingers in a fist please.
That's enough thanks! This vein is perfect.

Now tell me.
Do English teachers punctuate text messages?
Ah! I see.
But you do? Uh! Huh!
Of course!
Precision is a habit…
and meaning can hang on a comma after all.

What about you, Gautam?
You do?
Well that's no surprise: I mean,
what use is a gastroenterologist
who doesn't know colons inside-out!

…and I'm sure Mr G. here,
as he just drifted off into a field of dreams
would have been quietly reassured to hear
that his surgeon is a believer in precision;
is habitually precise!
No place for slapdash or near-enough here!

Canadian Rockies:
On a Rocky Mountain High

My eldest sister would like to know
if we have seen any Mounties in Canada!
Maybe she is hoping we will run into Nelson Eddy
riding over a mountain singing, "Indian Love Call"!

So I send her a picture of a grizzly
dressed in a Mountie uniform—hat and all;
And me leaning on his arm—old buddies;
enough to keep the romance alive for her.

And why not! There is romance enough here,
though rare bear-sightings are more common
than sightings of Mounties in uniform!
We have the digital photos to prove it!

The magic starts as our train pulls out of Banff
cruising along beside the beautiful Bow River;
a mirror for perfect reflections of peaks and trees:
Invert the picture and you won't know the difference!

And then the mighty Columbia takes up the baton
and we can't get enough of the colour:
aqua and turquoise in a tumble of rapids;
but be quick to snap the shot through the trees…

For trees, there are in extravagant abundance
interweaving their arms and shrouding the forest floor:
quivering aspens and firs, pines and spruce—
all competing for a foothold on precarious slopes.

Under the trees behold a bawdy abundance of berries
Colourful temptations for Bruno and other critters.
The train pulls into a siding, deferring to a freight train.
We'd rather we had stopped for a bear sighting!

Above the alpine tree-line arise ancient, craggy pyramids,
snow-capped masters of their heady domains;
the real heroes of our romance. Ah! The Rockies!
Full of surprises! Maybe a Mountie in costume
WILL serenade us around the next corner!

Germany:
Welcome to Dachau

Arbeit macht frei: working will make you free!
Those twisted words in wrought iron on the gate
Seemed promising enough at any rate
On entering protective custody.

"Protective custody"—the irony.
For Himmler's aim was to protect the state
From Jews, political dissenters, gays
For whom he had complete antipathy.

Thus very soon the prisoners found out
The only freedom they might find was death
For nothing could withstand the shibboleth
That fed the Nazi prejudice and hate.

The badge one wore depended on one's 'crime',
But all were put to work no matter what
And many inmates dropped dead on the spot
Forced labour used as torture on the sly.

What sort of mind devises such a place?
Heaters in rooms with the controls outside
To make those sweat in summer who'd defied
The guards or failed to self-efface!

And great coats with two pockets; but for certain
The punishment was harsh if one should dare
To warm one's hands or keep an item there:
The use of pockets was strictly verboten!

And medical experiments too were common
Like those devised by sadist Sigmund Rascher
Where inmates died of hypothermia
Or agonising rapid decompression.

Electric fences kept the prisoners in;
Dare step upon the grass there, you'd be shot
And some there were who chose this for their lot
Escaping from the hell that they were in.

Of sociopathic games one was the worst.
Soldiers devised this vile Catch 22,
Sad nemesis of many a gay and many a Jew;
And here is how the prisoners were coerced:

Soldiers would throw a cap onto the grass
And order some poor soul to pick it up.
To step upon the grass meant he'd be shot;
Refusing such an order meant no less!

Well may we think all this is in the past
But take a look at our world if you will
The sociopathic bullies are here still
Islamic State shows mankind at its worst.

And many bosses too lack empathy;
Targets and lists of outcomes rule their lives
And this is how employees are advised:
Do what we say with no integrity!

Arbeit macht frei: working will make you free!
The sociopath exists in every age;
So we must take a stance and vent our rage
To make the world a better place for you and me!

For only if we ALL step on the grass
And, risking bullets, seek to call them out
Will they realise there is not any doubt
Their actions will unleash the grapes of wrath.

Iceland:
Takk Fyrir Mig

Thank You from Me

When I was just a little boy, I thought Santa was real
But then I learnt Saint Nicholas was not quite the real deal!
So that meant Rudolph must be fake along with his red nose:
No different from the unicorns were reindeer I supposed.

But now we've been to Iceland and I'm starting to believe
'Cos here are things my wildest dreams could never have
        conceived:
Here reindeer really do exist, though seldom are they seen;
They just leave footprints in the snow to show where they
        have been!

We've seen volcanic lava fields so charged with mystery
It isn't hard to think of trolls as huge as huge can be,
Who partied all night long and then let out a mighty groan
'Cos when the sun shines on a troll, it quickly turns to stone.

So is it that in Dimmuborgir that you will quickly find,
If you study columns carefully, without a pre-set mind
It's not so hard to see a troll that's long been petrified.
Just take a look: that trolls once were just cannot be denied!

And elves are taken seriously; do not disturb their houses.
The route of highways can be changed by expert elf advisors.
Elves hide amongst the rocks, you see—and there are quite a
few!
(But whether elves and trolls get on I wouldn't have a clue.)

Oh, Iceland is quite magical, a land of ice and snow
For glaciers and ice caps will leave you gasping, "Wow!"
And countless water falls are born from all the melting ice,
Which waterfalls are grander than most others on the earth.

There are funny little critters that you wouldn't think could fly
But we've witnessed puffin magic with such critters whizzing
by.
Oh, I could go on and rave about so many other sights
(Including things, we've yet to see such as the Northern Lights).

Suffice to say that Iceland has exceeded expectations
And we would like to humbly thank our Icelandic relations
Sirry and Reynir who've unveiled its wonderful enticements.
Takk Fyrir Mig, "Thank you from me", for this time of
enchantment.

Politics Aside

Reflecting on Current Issues

20/20 Vision

Written on 15 December 2020

With 20/20 vision now, you'd think that we could see
Things that are bleeding obvious, with perfect clarity.
With 20/20 vision now, you'd think that, looking back,
We would have worked out what's gone wrong and so
      would learn from that!

With 20/20 vision now, we've watched the fires burn.
I wonder if we'll analyse; I wonder if we'll learn.
The RFS had warned the politicians months ago
Of looming Armageddon but they didn't want to know!

With 20/20 vision now, you'd think that we would know
That we must live in harmony and not trade blow for blow.
But wrathful men still stir up strife and, spurred by their conceit,
The mouths of fools' gush folly still[*]—though nowadays in a
      tweet!

---

[*] Proverbs 15:2

With 20/20 vision now, you'd think that we'd be wise
And not keep spewing toxic gases up into the skies.
Carbon emissions now exceed some thirty billion tonnes:
It doesn't take a scientist to know that that's not on!

With 20/20 vision now, you'd think we'd understand
Just how much ice is melting from the glaciers on
       Greenland:
300 gigatons a year! If a nod's as good as a wink,
Then ocean levels have to rise—faster than we might think!

With 20/20 vision now, you'd think we'd be aware
If visibility is low and dust storms fill the air
That clearing forests as we do, it really has to cease:
Worldwide each year the total cleared exceeds the size of
       Greece!

With 20/20 vision now, you'd think we'd realise
That it's not healthy if each meal is served with Coke and fries!
And smoking gives one lung cancer; it really isn't cool
So, if one keeps on smoking then one really is a fool!

With 20/20 vision now, you'd think that we would care
That plastic rubbish in our waters kills the sea life there.
With 20/20 vision now, it cannot be denied
That mass extinctions are in train; we should be horrified!

We've over-run the planet; we've gone forth and multiplied
Eight billion folk on spaceship earth is global suicide.
Our resources are limited and yet consumption grows;
Expansion economic models aggravate our woes!

With 20/20 vision now, we look back on a year
Affected by pandemic woes, and one thing's mighty clear:
We social distance, isolate when we have understood
Foregoing certain freedoms will advance the common good!

So, we must heed the prophets, pluck heads out of the sand
Observe the clues around us and try to understand
Unless our vision changes, unless we change the meme,
Our spaceship will face challenges like nothing ever seen!

Australians All

Australians all, it's time to start a sensible discussion
About when we should celebrate our bonding as a nation,
You see, some southern Councillors don't like our current
      date
And think that they can alter it without national debate!
It's fair enough that they should think that there should be a
      change
But is it their prerogative such things to rearrange?

So let us all reflect upon the current situation:
The 26th of January is causing some vexation.
That was the day that Arthur Phillip came to Sydney Cove.
(A few days spent at Botany Bay convinced him he should
      move).
But it wasn't until February that the Governor proclaimed
The colony of New South Wales—and this should be
      explained:

New South Wales went only to one thirty-five degrees,
Half way across the continent; and east, across the seas,
Included, notionally at least, what we now call New Zealand,
Though later, with a treaty, they became a separate free land

But as for mainland New South Wales, no treaty here
        occurred;
Because of lack of farming, *terra nullius* was declared.

In the sand dunes of Lake Mungo, there the evidence exists:
Aborigines have been here thirty thousand years at least!
And when white settlement occurred the impact was horrific:
Says Dunmore Lang, a grazier laced their damper with some
        arsenic.
Disease and shootings killed off more, so it is estimated
Indigenous Australians were quite literally decimated.

And New South Wales itself became an area fragmented
As other colonies were formed and rival tensions mounted
First Risdon Cove, Port Phillip Bay and in the West, Swan River
(A colony quite separate, a point one should consider!)
And in the north was Moreton Bay and south was South
        Australia.
Between the lot were rivalries, not obvious cohesion.
In no sense were the colonies united as a nation.

In the middle of the nineteen hundreds, there was little
        passion
For engaging in discussion on colonial federation
But then in eighteen eighty-nine, a Henry Parkes oration
Focused on uniting to enhance defensive options.

(Now the concept of a nation is a really abstract notion
And New Zealand and Fiji were both involved in first
discussions!)

And so, it was the colonies all held a referendum
And then the Commonwealth was born by royal proclamation
Australia as a nation now had finally begun:
Tuesday, the first of January, in Nineteen hundred and one.
That also was when states were born instead of colonies
So really that's the obvious date for our festivities!

So, Councillors, you have a case for changing what we do
But really, it's a national matter; it isn't up to you.
The current date is rather strange for many, many reasons,
Of which the most important is the aboriginal grievance,
For as it stands Australia Day connotes the fell occasion
That British subjects landed here and started an invasion!

So let us set this matter right in democratic fashion
For we are a democracy that acts through legislation.
The councillors are right to say a change of date is due
But it must be Australians all who vote, not just a few
So that in future everyone is happy to agree
The first day of the year is where Australia Day should be!

And while we're at it, let's repair our dodgy national anthem
So, everyone can sing it with equal enthusiasm
And 'girt by sea' is something of a curiosity
I'm sure we can do better; most people would agree.
I've given it a shot below, and really here's the thing,
I hope the words are better so Australians all can sing:

Australians all let us rejoice that we are living free
Within a democratic land based on equality.
Ours is an island continent of beauty rich and rare;
In history's page, let every stage Advance Australia Fair.
In joyful strains, then let us sing, Advance Australia Fair.

Beneath our radiant Southern Cross, we'll toil with hearts
*   and hands;*
To make this commonwealth of ours renowned of all the
*   lands;*
Our strength is our diversity, so let us all declare
That we will all endeavour to Advance Australia Fair.
In joyful strains, then let us sing, Advance Australia Fair.

Wugulora—One Mob!

Manus Island

Who among us in all truth has never taken flight
From wasps trying to sting us or a dog trying to bite
Or panicked waking from a dream that didn't turn out right?
Why is it then we cannot ken a refugee's sad plight?

Who has not fled the dark forest where loathsome creatures
      lurk:
Where Aragog's vast tribe of spiders send one's mind berserk;
And souls are sucked by death eaters, servants of Voldemort:
Only great fear prompts one to flee one's home as last resort!

What parent has not held a child throughout an endless night,
Fearing the worst but hoping that her illness will end right;
And tried to calm her anxious fears while they have held her
      tight.
Well, refugees are parents who just try to change their plight.

So why is it we live in fear and fail to understand
And keep them in detention camps with no hope near at hand
While we ignore them and prefer to hide our heads in sand
Instead of doing all we can to lend a helping hand?

Oh yes, I hear you now object, they've taken the back door
They haven't lined up in a queue; they've made a beeline for
Somewhere a family can live in peace for now and
evermore,
A place to live a life that you would give your right arm for;
(And some of them have done just that to grasp at any straw)
Well…seeking asylum is no crime; it's not against the law!

So when we hear of refugees whose lives are torn apart
Let not the fear of Aragog then harden up our heart
But let us think as parents who would give them a new start
And build a world where Manus Island cannot have a part!

The Modern Shock Jock

I am a modern shock jock: I speak what's on my mind!
I'm critical of anyone whose thoughts are not aligned
With my pontifications (I'm always right, you'll find)
So, listen up, dear listener, for I have an axe to grind!

I specialise in vitriol; my aim is to demean;
I like to talk in language that is blatantly obscene.
My mouth is full of verbiage not fit for the latrine
For there's nothing I like better than to really vent my
spleen.

I have a solemn duty to put people in their place
Especially politicians whom I think are a disgrace!
I give them a back-hander; yes, I slap them in the face
When I have finished with them, they will quickly fall from
grace!

And if you are a woman don't you dare to rock my boat
Or I'll tell you, "Put a sock in it" or ram one down your
throat!
Now I'm not misogynistic but I find a petticoat
Is more than I can handle and is sure to get my goat!

Enthroned behind my microphone I jaw and jaw and jaw
For to fill airwaves with hate speech is what I most adore.
I don't succumb to modesty for that would be a flaw.
I am a modern shock jock: I speak, my word is LAW!

Cool It!

You're a climate change denier so there's no more to be said
If you don't believe in climate change, you're not right in
      your head!
Now I may not be a scientist, but this I know for sure:
The seas are rising higher than they've ever been before!

I see! I see! I guess you're right but one thing puzzles me:
Just how far back in time have you read climate history?
The sea was much, much lower twenty thousand years ago;
It's come up nigh four hundred feet to be where it is now!

Sea rise and fall is nothing new and continents were joined:
The world was somewhat colder then and ice covered the
      land.
Across the Bering Land Bridge, folk from Siberia
Migrated eastward then turned south once they had reached
      Alaska.

You're a climate change denier; you should just accept the
    fact
That the polar ice is calving—how can you not react?
I've seen it on the TV and it really freaks me out:
That climate change is happening there clearly is no doubt.

Ah Yes! The ice is calving, but there's nothing new in that.
Recall Al Gore's prediction in the year two thousand and
    eight
That Greenland's ice would all be gone in five short years
    from then
And it did retreat significantly to half of what it's been.

But since that time, it has bounced back: Al Gore was wrong
    you know
And in Eastern Antarctica there's been a lot of snow
So, while there's carving in the West, the East is gaining
    weight
The ice is not depleting much, just altering its shape!

You're a climate change denier—after what we've just been
    through?
The evening news has shown these fires; we've had a front-
    seat view!
People have died, houses have burnt and animals have
    perished.
Can you deny that climate change is why the fires flourished?

The climate changes constantly; it has since the year dot
And yes, there have been bushfires and the year has been
>> *quite hot;*
But did you know that bigger bushfires happened here before
Just research nineteen thirty-nine and nineteen seventy-four!

Our hearts go out to everyone who's suffered in the fires;
But when our hearts are heavy, knee-jerk reactions aren't
>> *required.*
Australia is a dry country; we'd been through a long drought:
When lightning hit the tinder box, that brought the fires
>> *about.*
(The theory it was arsonists does simply not check out!)

Now! Now! Don't get excited! Most scientists agree
The world is hotter than it was—hotter by one degree;
But WHY the world is hotter is the subject of debate…
And frightened people close their ears, certain they are
>> *right.*

Political correctness often stifles depth of thought;
Political correctness has become a juggernaut!
Our life is full of new terms with a value-added twist
And when they're used, their clear intents to slap one on
>> *the wrist!*

And 'climate change denier' is the new kid on the block:
It casts a clear aspersion; it is clearly meant to mock,
Though what it is that gives so-called 'deniers' cause to pause
Is: they may acknowledge changes but debate what is the
>> *cause!*

Our eco-system is complex, the sub-systems diverse
Carbon dioxide and methane are on the rise of course;
But did you know that if you graph increase and temperature
The correlation's not direct; we need to take a breather!

145

There are lots and lots of reasons we should reduce the CO^2
It really isn't healthy; smog's blocking out the view!
But if one cast aspersions, if one attacks 'the man',
Perhaps it means one's arguments themselves are rather
*   bland!*

Name calling wins no arguments, it simply gives offence;
Perhaps 'denier' is a term with which we should dispense?
Emotion confounds argument—it really does confuse it:
The planet and the rhetoric –let's see if we can't cool it!

Computer Crash

What a lugubrious snail is this my ballpoint pen
I struggle to make meaning in its twisting trail
And yet, poets of old found ample eloquence
Scratching poetic meaning with ink pot and quill!

Why is it that I feel such disconnection
Now my computer keyboard offers no response?
What is this ball and chain that hinders composition
And slows my brain into a torpid somnolence?

The brain would rather leap with lithe agility
Partner to dancing fingers on the clattering keys
Swirling in verbal figures fertile in possibility,
Brain and fingers working with synchronous ease.

For what is composition if not the acrobatic brain
Processing words with skilful verbal legerdemain!

The Bullet-Spangled Banner

O say can you see, by the dawn's early light,
In a hail of gunfire more Americans dying
Who have all been assured to own guns is a right
And the Second Amendment is worth their defending?
Another night spent in fear, gunfire shattering the air,
Gives proof through the night that this lie is still there.
O say does the blinkered and the blind NRA
Still believe guns keep them free? Can they be so naïve!

O thus be it ever, when Americans stand
With a semi-automatic reeking more mass destruction
With gun power that can kill randomly on demand.
Damn the N.R.A. hold over all of the nation.
For succumb they all must when in their faces is thrust
The time-honoured motto: *In guns do we trust!*
So the star-spangled banner at half-mast again is raised
O'er a land that's far from free from the acts of the crazed!

War Against Want at Christmas

Of all the things my father taught me, this I value most:
That when we have our friends around and I am playing host
And organising drinks for them, a lager or a lite
Not to ask them what they *want* but rather what they'd *like*!

Now this may seem quite trivial, but our world is, I vow,
A world where people want and want (When do they want
it?
    NOW!)
And 'want' is a self-centred word; it's not at all polite,
As if the wanting in itself creates a human right!

Computer programs are at fault; they reinforce the meme.
They ask us what we *want* to do; and, swimming with the
    stream,
We copy what we hear each day without the slightest notion
That word choice shapes our character through subtle
    connotation.

So, food tastes much, much better at a favourite restaurant
When waiters ask what one would *like* and not 'What do you
      whaant?'
Or likewise on the radio, the host who tells a guest
She'd *like* to ask a question displays civil courteousness.

And so this Christmas let us ask a child what s/he would like
Santa Claus to bring her in her stocking Christmas night
For then, the child can understand that when we make a wish
It is just that, something we'd *like* and, if received, a gift.

Mr Putin's Christmas Cards

Forgive me, Mr Putin, but I'm wondering, Vladimir,
Just what will you be writing on your Christmas cards this
year?
Will the theme be, "Peace on earth and goodwill to all
men"?
And will you call to mind a child once born in Bethlehem?

You appear to be a Christian; well, you wear a crucifix,
And you're often seen with clerics who are Russian
      Orthodox.
Are you just playing politics or are you quite sincere?
Cos *Love Thy Neighbour*'s a commandment you don't seem
      to hear!

Thou shalt not kill's another one; the cross you wear's a
sham.
Your moral compass is deranged; you fail to understand
That while you think you're powerful, that you are quite the
      man,
Your place in history will be writ as someone to be damned.

Attending Christmas services, just what will be your
prayers?
Will you ask that God protect your children and your heirs?
Or on the altar of your cause, like prophet Abraham,
Will you offer up your daughters as your stance demands?
Will you give thanks for soldiers killed in this most awful
war,
Two hundred thousand Russians dead, at least that, maybe
        more?
And will their mothers and their fathers say a loud 'Amen!'
Or will their tears inform you of a grief too deep to pen?

Forgive me, Mr Putin, but, I'm wondering, Vladimir,
Just what will you be writing on your Christmas cards this
        year?
Will you have an epiphany, and join the world refrain?
Peace on the earth, goodwill to men—and that includes
        Ukraine!